To

our Nancy

WHEN TRAGEDY STRIKES

CHARLES B. GRAVES, JR.

MOODY PRESS

CHICAGO

© 1972 by
Crescendo Book Publications
Dallas, Texas

MOODY PAPERBACK EDITION, 1976

Library of Congress Cataloging in Publication Data
Graves, Charles B   1926-
    When tragedy strikes.
    1. Consolation. I. Title.
BV4905.2.G7   1976   242'.4   75-29016
ISBN 0-8024-9429-3

All Scripture quotations, except where indicated otherwise,
are from the New American Standard Bible. © The Lock-
man Foundation, 1960, 1962, 1963, 1971, 1973.

Printed in the United States of America

Contents

Prologue

"Lord, who can be just but Thou only?" The rush-hour traffic was heavy, as usual; and, as usual, I thought of the nearness of death. I thought of the powerful engine that responded so readily as the freeway traffic surged, of its power to destroy (Was it 50,000 lives last year?), of its power to add dimension to the lives of 200 million Americans. And then—like all else in life—I saw the mixture of good and evil. And I thought of man, who so inadequately separates the two, if indeed he knows the difference.

"Lord, I didn't really want to be on this jury, let alone be its foreman. Tomorrow I must have an opinion: Who was at fault?" It seemed such a small matter, a relatively minor civil suit arising from a traffic accident. But what of the man who claimed he could no longer work? That he could no longer support his family? No small thing for him. That's a terrible price. And, if out of carelessness, or even coincidence, whose fault was it? Who pays? An insurance company probably, but what does that matter? There's right, and there's wrong.

Anyway, tomorrow I must reach that decision. Then again that feeling, "But, God, only Thou art wise." Perhaps that's why we have juries. There must be more of God in twelve of us than in one. God in us, how else can man judge or rule or even live?

At last I was home. I saw Nancy was gone, probably to take her grandmother home to nearby Georgetown. I did wish she'd not go by way of that terrible intersection, with the treacherous left turn across busy US 183. But then, she had a point in saying that the construction along the other route was dangerous too.

It's always interesting to find which of the children are at home. Loving children make every workday a real homecoming, and sharing time begins at once. Marcia was there; at fourteen she wouldn't have gone with her mother—and leave the telephone! And Maurine, at almost ten, naturally preferred the quiet of home over the busy family station wagon.

The others were willing travelers; Chip, at twelve, wouldn't refuse a ride, if just to back out of the driveway. And Nancy Lu, at seven, like her mother, was always where the action was. And Carolyn, just nineteen months, went everywhere her mother went.

Home is where the heart is, and our home includes a place of meditation, a wellspring of communion with our God. It serves our spirits one by one or in groups of two or more. No home can be complete without an altar to the living God. In some homes it may be a hearth or a table on which the family Bible rests. For other families a quiet garden is more appropriate, and for our family it is a creek named Little Walnut. This is our living altar, so like our lives, usually serene and peaceful, but occasionally almost dry, barren, and under a seemingly merciless summer sun. And then, at other times, it becomes a raging torrent, untamed and free. Like life, that sometimes moves too fast, it can scarcely be contained within its usual channel. But in a few hours its rage is spent; and in its devastated valley it is small again, picking its way through its own debris in search of the serenity it knew before the storm.

Maurine went out with me to explore our altar, so near the busy freeways, yet so far from man's creations and so close to God's.

Our sojourn was interrupted by not-so-distant sirens, and I felt a tug, for I knew someone was in trouble. And another tug came from deeper within me, and I sensed that we were involved. The spell was broken; and I returned, thoughtful but not especially concerned, to the house, leaving Maurine in her beloved outdoors.

Back inside, it was Marcia who answered an insistent telephone and reluctantly surrendered it to her father. Just eight words and I knew my faith was on trial: "Mr. Graves, have you heard about the wreck?" Even as my heart responded, I felt God's promise: "Yea, though I walk through the valley of the shadow of death," and I felt His strength.

My voice asked, "Where?" and "Are they all right?" My heart soared as she said, "They think the children are all right," then plunged as she added, "But they don't know about the women."

There was no way to prepare Marcia. I could only say, "They've had a wreck, a bad one. Get Maurine quickly." I had asked the location, knowing it would be the intersection of US 290 and US 183. I was compelled to go first to the nearby scene, as though I must satisfy myself that the ambulance had left no one there. In just minutes we viewed Nancy's pride and joy, her long-awaited new white station wagon, impacted at the driver's door and horribly crushed.

The girls knew; they had to know. I looked at the wooden faces of the gathered onlookers. They knew. The scene was as quiet as a hospital corridor; the feel of sudden death was heavy.

With the simple prayer, "Take over now,

Lord," I turned the car and began the long journey to the emergency room. Neither Marcia nor Maurine was hysterical, as both bowed their heads and prayed with me through the seemingly interminable dash to gather up what remained of a family that had long thrived on God's abundant blessings. We prayed first that we would behave as His servants, accepting His will, that He would make a testimony out of the experience we were now entering. We prayed for each of our loved ones that had ridden into the tragedy. We prayed for Grandma Shug, Nancy's paternal grandmother, at eighty-four a choice servant of God. Surely no one ever bestowed more love on our family. How she idolized our golden-voiced Nancy. They did so many things for one another. Even as we prayed for her, I knew she couldn't bear to survive this precious daughter of her only son. Then we prayed for Nancy, and how we prayed for a wife and mother of such rare quality! We resolved together that we would try to match in this moment her great faith. Then, for each of the children, and for all of them, and for all of us. We prayed for the other driver, and we prayed for those who would be receiving them by now at the hospital—for the doctors and the nurses.

At last we were there, parking quickly and running, not wanting to know and desperately needing to be with them. I declared our name as we burst on the scene. Everyone was busy. I saw Chip first, bleeding, uncrying, disturbed, but patient as attendants worked over him. He understood as we moved on to Nancy Lu, unbloodied and marvelously controlled for her seven years. They brought little Carolyn, scarcely conscious but hopefully all right, no broken limbs but with obvious head injuries. Marcia moved quickly to tend little Carolyn as she was taken for X rays, and Maurine silently joined Nancy Lu. Chip had to go alone for his X rays as I pressed a raging, burning question, from which they all turned: "How about my Nancy? When can I see her? Are the doctors with her now? How bad is she?"

Finally an administrator came and, on verifying my identity, said simply, "Both the women were dead on arrival."

I was not unprepared. The strength I had prayed for surged, as I thought, *Even now she is with our blessed Lord. She knows no pain, nor ever will again.* Now I prayed, "Lord, make me a minister to my children, to Nancy's family, to mine, and to all her host of friends," and again, "Begin now to show through us the all-sufficiency of Thy grace."

As the children were returned, I asked that they let me bring them together for a few moments; they must know quickly. Attendants seemed distressed that I'd not wait for our pastor. And then I was face to face with our five precious children, and I knew that Nancy had left much of herself.

As the children heard from me the simple truth that their mother was gone and could not return, her faith shined as brightly as the sun through each one. There were tears, of course, but only for a moment, as they bowed with me and thanked God for the beautiful life Nancy had known, beautiful because it was lived so close to Him. We thanked Him for the privileged years we had shared with her. And we thanked Him for Shug, and for all she had been to us. There was no doubt in their eyes as we agreed that both Nancy and Shug were all right now. I and the children, even at their tender years, knew that death now held fresh promise for us: reunion.

We knew they were even now reunited with Nancy's father, Shug's son, and surely the angels sang. And we said another prayer for ourselves. We committed ourselves to their memory and, most of all, to live our lives, more than ever before, that He might be glorified.

We lifted up our eyes, and I surveyed the children who would carry on for their mother the ministry of love that is their heritage. She had taught them well, and her mission was obviously in good hands as our bedraggled, bandaged, and heartbroken little band opened the doors to meet the world. Everyone knew that the faint smiles we wore were no mark of irreverence but the very imprint of peace that "our trust is in the Lord."

The ensuing hours, days, and months were times of revelations. With tender and receptive hearts born of deepest tragedy, God's comforting lessons came loud and clear. From His holy Book, from hours of quiet meditation, from times of sharing with loved ones possessing boundless faith—from all these have come a fresh and magnificent insight of God and His purposes.

The true meaning of the peace that passes all understanding, and the lessons and the discoveries of that peace as magnified by Nancy's passing from this life are described in these pages which make up my book.

1

Peace

Now may the Lord of peace Himself continually grant you peace in every circumstance. The Lord be with you all!

2 THESSALONIANS 3:16

Peace is the golden dream of a stricken world. It is a dream that paralyzes some and activates others. Some men and most nations would pay any price for an era of peace. Many would die to achieve it, yet they cannot define it. Peace is recommended by those who have never experienced it and generously offered by those who cannot produce it. It is demanded by those who profess a belief only in what one can see, taste, hear, or feel. Ironically, this day's rising clamor for peace, backed by increasing violence and anarchy, constitutes a growing threat to a somewhat orderly society of man.

15

A popular concept of peace is well demonstrated by the response of a four-year-old, fresh from an encounter in a church nursery. When asked to explain his attack on little Johnny, his rejoinder was an authoritative, "I'm gonna teach that kid to 'Be ye kind.' "

There are those to whom peace means simply having one's own way. This is the spoiled child's anarchistic drive so prominently featured about today's world.

To the apathetic, peace is merely "being left alone." A self-centered existence, denying reality, resents the intrusions of the world. The disciple of apathy is convinced that, if his own small world could completely shut out the big bad world with all its problems, instant peace would be his.

To so many, peace means the absence of struggle against conflict, against material want, against disease and suffering. It would mean total, perpetual comfort and would (if this were indeed the substance of peace) wipe out in one stroke all the accomplishments and progress of man since God's early admonishment:

And God blessed them, and God said unto them, Be fruitful, and multiply, and replenish the earth, and subdue it: and have dominion over the fish of the sea, and over the

16

*fowl of the air, and over every living thing
that moveth upon the earth.*

GENESIS 1:28 (KJV)

The concept of peace that rejects struggle is more befitting to the now extinct species of animals than to man, who is made in God's own image.

To perhaps most people, "peace" is a word used interchangeably with "truce." A truce is a standoff; this is not so of true peace. Many a marriage that is thought to be peaceful is nothing more than a truce. A truce depends on a balance of powers, and is therefore usually referred to as shaky or uneasy.

Peace is positive, permanent, and unshakable. A truce is arranged by force, by politics, by pleading or cajoling; or it is purchased at great expense or given by generous and benevolent powers. But, if a truce is arranged, purchased, or given, then it follows that the same truce can be disarranged, sold, or taken back.

Peace is like charity, beginning in the person who desires it. It is not forced on others, wished on others, or sold to others. And contrary to popular political promises, peace cannot be cast like a net over large or small segments of a complex society.

Peace can never come to one who does not desire it; it is unattainable for one who denies its source. The only peace anyone can realize is his own. We can speak to others of peace, even inspire them to pursue it. But if this inspiration is to be real and productive, we must speak from a personal knowledge and understanding. We must define peace, first knowing it ourselves, and must point to its one real source if we wish to share it.

Yet, just what is real peace? What is the true nature of peace, and what is its origin? It will come as a shock to many that peace can and does coexist with war, that peace can and does accompany suffering, and that genuine peace can and does stand close beside great personal tragedy. One of life's most cruel hoaxes is the belief that the banishment of something or other, or its absence or nonexistence, is the prerequisite of peace.

Peace is a positive force, not a negative condition. It is not the mere absence of life's problems small and great. Indeed, peace can be likened to light. The darkness within which men grope is dark only because of the absence of light. The darkness is the negative, and the light positive. Can darkness subdue light? Of course not; nor can troubled times subdue real peace.

When we find the light in a once darkened room, its coming does not banish the furniture over which we stumbled; it only illuminates it and gives us the ability to see it and to avoid the painful consequence of stumbling. And so peace is the inner quality that lights the possessor's way. It serves, not to banish those things in life's way over which one might stumble but to shed over them a light of understanding, that we might avoid or overcome them.

This peace is the substance of the well-known prayer of Reinhold Niebuhr: "O God, give us serenity to accept what cannot be changed, courage to change what should be changed, and wisdom to distinguish the one from the other."

The darkness of an "empty" room would hardly need a light, for there would be no obstacles. And a life lived with no problems, no trials, no wants—if such a ridiculous state were even possible—would have no need for peace. But no life can be completely free from want; for, even if a utopian existence could come to pass, man would still face physical death.

Because man, the creature, can never banish his own needs, God, the Creator, gave us His own Son, Jesus Christ, the light in the otherwise darkened room of the inner man. Christ is the peace positive to troubled man, and there is no other such force. Nor can man, with all his God-given skill, ever hope to invent another. And this peace positive, Jesus Christ our Lord, is unlike the counterfeit peace man wars for, begs for, riots for, and demands from governments; this is the one and only attainable peace, for its origin and source is our very God.

Many have attained this peace and at all times possess this peace, but no one has achieved a different peace by any other means. Those who claim an alien peace live, at best, with a truce, a temporary and delicate balance which will never withstand the realities of life and death.

The time came suddenly and unexpectedly for me to test the ability to "give thanks to God for all things." No mere balance could have substituted for the unassailable peace beyond understanding as I stood before the stilled form of my beloved Nancy, the selfless, talented mother of our five children—my Nancy who just hours before had been vibrant, alive, and the unquestioned possessor of this peace. And I found it not hard to say, "Thank You, God," and "God, make me, even as she, an instrument of Thy peace." And I knew afresh, and as never before, that the peace I knew was real and unassailable. It had passed the test on lesser occasions, in a personal sense. It had seen me through two wars, through personal conflicts, through fear, through natural and man-made disasters, through physical injury, through the needs, dangers, and turmoil that are man's lot; and now through far more than all these, doubled and redoubled, into separation from one dearer far than life.

I can imagine yet a greater test than this, but only one: the separation by death from a loved one who had never discovered peace. To stand at the grave of a loved one who has died in darkness, who can never know the light, to whom peace is forever beyond reach, and who will never know the presence of a living God—this would be a harsher test.

Our beloved Nancy beheld the Light that took her from our presence. She lives today in a place of perfect and lasting peace, and I'll see her there when our Lord calls me from this place. We are separated but for a time.

I pray that I might so witness to my remaining loved ones that my peace will never be subjected to the test of eternal separation from a loved one. But, if such a test must come, I'm confident that even then the peace that comes from God will endure.

It has come to me that our Lord Jesus Christ experienced at one point the hell that we who serve Him will never encounter. He experienced it for our sakes and expressed it on the cross when,

And about the ninth hour Jesus cried out with a loud voice, saying "Eli, Eli, lama

21

SABACHTHANI?" *that is,* "MY GOD, MY GOD, WHY HAST THOU FORSAKEN ME?"

MATTHEW 27:46

Only at this moment in history has one, having once known the peace of God, found it taken away. God turned His back on His own Son, taking away His very presence, His peace. And He took it away for our sakes, that, once we have accepted it, His peace will never fail us. In that moment, Jesus experienced loss beyond that ever to be known by any other. For having known peace, He was without it. Men without peace do not know how great it is, for they have never known it. And anyone, once he has known peace, can never lose it, as our Lord did for us even as He hung on the cross.

For I am convinced that neither death, nor life, nor angels, nor principalities, nor things present, nor things to come, nor powers, nor height, nor depth, nor any other created thing, shall be able to separate us from the love of God, which is in Christ Jesus our Lord.

ROMANS 8:38-39

2

"God's Will" Power

So many times we encounter embittered survivors of deep personal tragedies, particularly those tragedies that involve the loss of loved ones. Many are bitter even toward God, presuming, it would seem, to judge Him and His management of His own creation. Often when confronted by friends questioning a tragic loss, we were unable to convey a satisfying answer.

One of the blessings that God has given to me out of our tragedy is the experience that identifies me with others suffering loss, and out of this experience I have been granted acceptable authority to apply God's Word to the frequent, agonized questions growing out of the death of loved ones.

And I realized that death is something we all must face and that we can avoid the loss by death of our loved ones only by preceding them to the grave. The more I considered these simplest of truths, the more fully I realized that God had given me, in my fresh experience, the added purpose of ministering to those who cry out an agonizing, heartrending, "Why?"

The sharing of any experience, be it happy or tragic, tends to establish something of a bond between those who share it. I have often felt that this bond, since our death experience, undiminished and even heightened, in the passing years. And to make a profitable bond for God's purposes, and in hopes of comforting and encouraging others, I have prayed and searched for the means of expressing those factors that comfort and encourage me so abundantly.

My immediate discovery in this search came as I gathered our children about me there in the hospital to share with them the fearful depth of our tragedy. I knew then that I had to be prepared in advance, that there was no longer time to seek the answers to explain our loss to myself or to the children.

The Bible study that Nancy and I had so often shared, the prayers, the open conversations about the certainty of death and the equal certainty of the life beyond the grave—these things had constituted our learning process. The subsequent confrontation with her death was the laboratory equivalent, the test, the proof. How could I possibly have performed in the laboratory of reality without the benefit of previous study of the text-book, the Bible, and the benefit of classroom discussions with Nancy?

I know now that I was prepared by a gracious, provident God for what I faced. With the very real presence of God's Spirit, even Nancy Lu, confident at just seven years, understood; and there was no destructive resentment within us from the very first till now.

I would say to any parent today, "If you are not prepared to shut yourself in a room alone with your children and tell them that Mother (or Daddy) is gone, and can't come back to them, then you have some serious homework to do." I thank God that my homework was done. I know now that our children's whole future depended on that fact.

I cannot now conceive of facing that experience unprepared and holding any shred of hope for a full psychological recovery of myself or the children.

And what of those who have neglected their homework? What of those who refused to face the reality of death until they were confronted by it? For the departed one, the answer is simple; for there are but two possibilities: either he has gone to be with the Lord he accepted while yet living, or he has gone to a place of eternal torment. Absolutely nothing can change that fact—no one's prayers, however fervent, no eulogy (this is man's evaluation, not God's), no power however great. The issue is settled and the result is irrefutable.

So, concern must obviously lie with the survivors. Any meaningful effort must be directed to the survivor's benefit; and, if the survivor was unprepared for the tragedy, he or she will need all the spiritual support that loving, thoughtful friends can muster. The prepared survivor can climb the mountain alone if need be; because, in the embrace of God's Spirit, he is never really alone. Nevertheless, the love and care expressed by friends in time of grief afford a buoyancy that can literally float one to the mountaintop. The memory of the loving deeds of so many gentle folk—my friends and Nancy's friends, some not even known to us—will be with me always. Even now I feel a residual strength from the great host who came to us in our time of need.

But, again, what of the unprepared survivor? What are the answers to his inevitable questions? God's will is questioned by mortal man because men fail, or often refuse, to understand what God's will is, or why. Theological expertise on the subject of God's will is available by the volume. The satisfying concept of God's will that has sustained us through the years comes from a single volume, the Holy Bible, and is supported first by prayer and discussion then by great and small testings.

A good many years ago Nancy and I agreed that God's will can be divided into two parts: His directive will and His permissive will. On the basis of this division, we have been able to accept all that this life has to offer. I know that I could have accepted Nancy's death even if I was certain God had directed it. But our merciful, loving Father did no such thing; instead, He permitted it.

Gravity is directed by God, as is the very beat of the heart. God has directed the environment within which the heart will beat, and has directed that it must, among other things, be amply supplied with good blood and function interdependently with an unbelievably complex nervous system, all created by Him. In fact, what generally is referred to as nature is the directive will of God.

The staunchest atheist glibly speaks of the laws of the universe, and agnostics speak in awe of the mysterious forces of nature. No accident here, of course, and no mystery; but rather, the work of the master Architect, a universe marvelously in tune and functioning by a flawless, intricate design! All mankind wonders at this delicately balanced but ruggedly reliable world in which we live. Too often man, the creature, overwhelmed by the marvels he sees about him, finds himself strangely committed to the creation rather than to the Creator. This created universe, unlike a great painting, a great accomplishment of inventive skill, a great book, or any other product of human genius, cannot and will not survive its Creator. This universe is no memorial to the Almighty, but it is unimpeachable evidence of His presence then, now, and forever.

The men most determined to limit God are often dedicated to proving the unlimited nature of God's creative work. What a sad and terrible contradiction to find in the judgment of any mortal! Yet it is a quirk to be found in the minds of some of the world's foremost scholars.

At that time Jesus answered and said, "I praise Thee, O Father, Lord of heaven and earth, that Thou didst hide these things from the wise and intelligent and didst reveal them to babes.

MATTHEW 11:25

How sad it is that learned men in their search for the secrets of creation can overlook the great, freely given truths of the Creator Himself and His love for man, His creature.

God's perfect directed will implies His perfect permissive will. For, if He directs that the hu-

28

man body must be sustained by blood and if He directs that the blood must be moved by the work of the heart through a network of arteries and veins, then He permits the flow to cease when the heart ceases to pump, and He permits life, as we know it, to cease as well. To do otherwise would be to repeal His perfect and directed will. And in such fashion came the death of our Nancy by God's will, His permissive will, because the car in which she sat was struck by another car traveling at great speed. God's directive will, by virtue of His laws of force, of gravity, and of body function, ruled her from this life.

For these same rules we can only give thanks to our God, for the universe as we know it could not exist without them. What a strange and unbearable circumstance it would be if these laws were switched on and off at random! A moment's thought should be sufficient for man to accept the reality that the unsurpassed strength of God's law, His will, is in its unfailing performance. And, when God made man free to choose, He certainly intimated no freedom from the consequences of his choice.

Nancy and I together, as we greeted our blessed children into this magnificent world, knowing that they, too, were God's creations, marveled and praised Him for His goodness, as revealed to us and bestowed on us through His perfect will. And we savored the things of God, not only His physical creations but even more the spiritual bonanza that comes with His lordship over our lives. Together we praised His will, we sought to honor it, and we pledged together to uphold it always before our children. And for all this and through the presence of His peace, I stood beside Nancy's fresh grave, in the presence of no one but God's Spirit, and found it neither difficult nor irrational to say, "Thank You, God, for Your just and perfect will."

3

Twice Charged

In the course of the years, Nancy and I had learned the singular power of God's Word. We had never found a problem in our lives to which the Bible did not address itself. Let me be quick to confess that I was never as faithful to study His Book as was Nancy. Her well-marked, well-used Bible will remain one of the most fitting tributes to her.

Our bookshelves are liberally stocked with modern translations, commentaries, and expository works, all to the end that we might together delve deeper and deeper into the living Word of God. Nancy was so dedicated to the pursuit of truth and the building of this library of life, that I frequently found myself busy building still more bookshelves.

In 1965, Nancy had given me a new marked reference Bible to aid my study and my teaching efforts. That Bible is now, of course, a double treasure. Very soon after our tragedy, while turning thoughtfully through this volume, I noticed for the first time on its flyleaf a scripture reference Nancy had left me. This note is in a different ink from her 1965 note of presentation. It was undated. In fact, it appeared quite fresh. Knowing Nancy, I deduced that she probably had been struck by the message of the text and, as was her habit, had appropriated it for me. Imagine the feeling within me as I read the freshly underscored words in my Bible, left for me by my faithful and beloved wife now so suddenly gone to be with our Lord. The feeling was heightened by the very significant fact that, as frequently as Nancy made notes in her own Bible, she had always refrained from marking mine.

I traced thoughtfully the familiar words, now carrying a fresh impact and a challenging mandate from beyond the very grave itself:

I thank my God upon every remembrance of you, always in every prayer of mine for you all making request with joy, for your fellowship in the gospel from the first day until now; being confident of this very thing, that he which hath begun a good work in you will perform it until the day of Jesus Christ. . . . And this I pray, that

your love may abound yet more and more
in knowledge and in all judgment; that ye
may approve things that are excellent; that
ye may be sincere and without offence till
the day of Christ; being filled with the fruits
of righteousness, which are by Jesus Christ,
unto the glory and praise of God. [The un-
derscore is Nancy's.]

PHILIPPIANS 1:3-11 (KJV)

I read the text again and again; and the meaning took on added dimension, for, coming to me
as it did, even if Nancy had shouted this message
from beyond the grave, it would have been no
more personal. This was her message—though it
was appropriated from Paul—and it said to me
that my work was not over and that the fruits of
her work would continue as well. I felt a very
strong sense of escalated responsibilities: my own
works, the continuance of hers, and the realization of dreams we'd dreamed together.

How many times we had prayed, "Lord, if
tragedy ever comes to our family, if it can be Thy
will, allow one of us—either of us—to remain
with our children till they are mature and secure
in the faith that sustains us." We could pray in
this fashion because we were "become one" to
the extent that I cannot recall even one serious

33

difference between us in our interpretation of God's Word or of its application to our lives.

As difficult and unpleasant as we knew separation would be, we had known that either of us could speak confidently for both. If both of us should be taken, though, we found it hard to imagine our young and growing children alone, at grips with a sinful world. Our most frequent prayer was that God would make of each of our children all that He had intended them to be. And we wanted the privilege of having a part in the process, having long since dedicated each of them to the Lord and to His service to the fullest extent that a parent can.

My charge was now quite clear, not a new charge perhaps but certainly under new conditions. God's words were clear; Nancy's admonishment was vivid. Together they said, "Adjust, grow, serve, and these through love." It was plain that the charge called for action now. There could be no delay for preparation, no time for self-pity or resentment, certainly no time for bitterness. I know Nancy would have considered such negative reactions a failure on my part and a contradiction to our life together and our plans.

Mourning must inevitably have its place, and there was an unfamiliar and lonesome quality with that great gulf now freshly separating us.

But mourning could not be allowed to dominate lest it become simply a surrender to emotion. And mourning could so easily have become a contradiction to the hope we shared. Her heart was still, but mine now beat for us both; the same Spirit that guided us together, still led the lonesome survivor.

Should life slow down? Seeing that our plans, purposes, and goals were not severed in half as we had been, what could my life do but take on an increasing sense of urgency? Indeed, all the elements of the renewed charge, "Adjust, grow, serve, and these through love," were magnified with each passing day. Our tragedy served not as a brake on the events of my life but rather as an accelerator. And in that acceleration lay much of the victory over the otherwise debilitating effects of mourning. We've long heard it said that the best prescription for overcoming sorrow and disappointment is to "get busy and stay busy." How true that saying is, but how grossly understated.

God energizes, or charges, each of His children, and He recharges us even as a battery is recharged. This recharging can be a painful experience, but even so it is God's reminder of whose we are and that there is a purpose to life. God has provided a way to avoid the necessity of life's rechargings. The battery of the Christian life can be kept strong and productive through the generative power of His Holy Spirit. When we neglect our prayer life, when we shun God's Word, when we forfeit that fellowship of the Spirit, then it is that we break contact with the great generator Himself. The power that comes from the Christian life, like the energy from the storage battery, is only coming out of storage. Neither the battery nor the Christian can create; they can only call out of storage a limited quantity of power for a limited time, unless there is a renewing from another source. And therein lies one great secret of the effective Christian life—the real *power source*. The power that resides in us is not ours; we are only the stewards, the storekeepers, the storage batteries. The power is God's own; it comes to us through contact with His Holy Spirit. And if we are so unwise as to neglect the ministry of His Spirit, we break the contact, forfeiting the renewing power.

When we shut off the power source and our limited supply is drained away, we very quickly become weak and ineffective. We begin to doubt; we discover fear; and we become empty, powerless, fragile vessels. I find too many of my Christian friends in this unhappy state today. Powerless, castaway by their own choice, adrift without that one connection that gives meaning to life, they have forfeited that fellowship with the Spirit. So many seem to have lost all hope. Their joy is gone, life is admittedly a drag, and they become weaker and sadder.

But God has provided, and that provision is as simple as it is wonderful. The Christian needs only to renew fellowship with his Maker. He needs to return to that moment when he accepted our Christ as Lord of his life. Maybe he never really knew that one must attach himself to the power source, the Holy Spirit. Maybe he thought God would give him his own generative power. Or perhaps, even after knowing the satisfaction of the wonderful inflowing power, he carelessly neglected the hookup and carelessly broke the connection that God never breaks. All this we call "being out of fellowship with God."

And in my days of maximum sensitivity, in the freshness of my sorrow, I found the cables strongest. I felt the surge of God's own power into this mortal vessel, and I found a strength not mine. I discovered how great a trust He grants when He charges and recharges us with that power.

God's charge, through the Spirit, is an enabling force. Nancy's charge, from the grave, was a call to use that force to "Adjust, grow, serve, and these through love." And as I considered these two charges, they merged together and I discovered my ministry. My ministry from the time of this revelation has been to do all that I can to lead God's children who linger on the fringe of His fellowship and lack the joy of serving Him to rediscover the power source, to draw freely from it, and to serve Him gladly. Then, and only then, will one discover, or rediscover, the real meaning of life. This happy exciting ministry I call my "fringe ministry." This is my charge.

4

Treasures

Do not lay up for yourselves treasures upon earth, where moth and rust destroy, and where thieves break in and steal. But lay up for yourselves treasures in heaven, where neither moth nor rust destroys, and where thieves do not break in or steal; for where your treasure is, there will your heart be also.

MATTHEW 6:19-21

I made the strange discovery in the aftermath of Nancy's death that I was unexpectedly happy and genuinely thankful for a small bank balance and for the fact that I had no large or small financial investments. What a comfort it was to confront the fact that we, almost unaware of the consequences, had invested all of our material resources in those things that enriched our contemporary years and in those things that were then

39

and are now in God's great storehouse. I have been spared the burden of accepting alone the dividends from investments we might have made together at the expense of sharing together God's material blessings. This does not imply a sense of wrongness in saving for the future, only that there are more important considerations. But how wrong it would seem now, to have asked Nancy to sacrifice those material pleasantries for the hope of future riches she never lived to enjoy.

God blessed us materially to the extent that as we moved successively to Dallas, to Fort Worth, and finally to Austin, Nancy was able to enjoy selecting, moving into, and making our home of three different new houses. Certainly none were mansions, but she loved them and what they could mean to our family. Her touch made each house our palace. I was always able to provide her with a means of transportation, and how she loved to drive. Surely half her driving miles or more were to or from the home of someone to whom she ministered. I couldn't buy her all the clothes she would have liked, but she never complained. Nancy was a beautiful woman, and her good taste included fashion. She always dressed her children and herself well, even on a slim budget. She made many of the clothes our children wore, and not a few of her own.

We always ate well, for Nancy loved to cook. This was in fact one of the many ways in which she lavished her love on us all. My still ample weight remains a testimony to her culinary ability, and I'm not sure I'll ever taste the equal of her lime pie.

Nancy gave all that she had as often as she could to assist in worthy causes, to encourage those in need, or just to show someone that somebody cares.

All this meant the bank balance usually read something like $1.17 by payday. So precarious was her balance, in fact, that we more than once paid penalties for returned checks. And yet, I never found her really foolish in her money management, and she certainly never overspent for herself. At any rate, all this meant no leftovers for financial investments. Any financial investment would have meant something we had spent otherwise would have been forgone. And in retrospect, I wouldn't trade a dime she used for a thousand shares of the richest stock on today's market.

Nancy and I learned early in our life together that there was but one way to bring God's tithe into His storehouse. Early in our marriage we were paid monthly, and we returned God's tithe in weekly increments, or at least that was our intention. But by the third week, or certainly by

41

the fourth, it was not a choice of whether we ate or paid our tithe. There was often not enough for our tithe even if we did forgo eating. It was then that we decided we must give to God monthly, as He gave to us and while the balance was adequate.

For the first few months we tried tithing monthly, it still didn't work, because as bills were paid at month's end, the new balance dropped menacingly. It was obvious that we could not write a check for a tenth and have any hope of feeding our children through the month. It was then that Nancy said, in near despair, "God will wait but our creditors won't." But, even as she spoke those words, she knew that wouldn't do either. Finally we found the faith to take the plunge that set our basic investment pattern in God's work through His Church. This pattern was rooted in the very simple decision to require of ourselves that the first check written after a bank deposit was for a full 10 percent of that paycheck, before deductions, and the check was made out to our local church there in Dallas, later in Fort Worth, and still later in Austin.

We never deviated from that decision, and we knew that it was one of the most meaningful we ever made. I'm sure that our spiritual growth really began at that point, and God's blessings flowed until we were scarcely able to receive them all—not material riches, but good health, beautiful children, a superabundance of good friends, and a shared inner satisfaction that we were participating in the greatest investment program known to man. And as participants we were in the largest investment club in the world, one with the singular purpose of advancing God's Kingdom throughout the world.

And at her death, no will was needed to pass to me Nancy's share of the investment, because suddenly she was much closer to the treasure than I.

And in the aftermath of our tragedy—in the mixture of mourning the separation and enjoying the memory of the blessed years—I came, belatedly, upon another revelation. We mortals are so naive when it comes to our own goodness! No credit is due Nancy and me for the tithes we brought; the good life that ensued was not because we had assumed a generous position, nor was it because we ourselves had become good. On the contrary, we had merely found out and turned from one sin. We were no longer stealing from God. God blessed us because we had repented the sin of misappropriating to our own use the tenth that was His. No longer burdened over the sin, we found a new and brighter fellowship together and most of all with God. It was at this point that we learned what it was not only to give but to receive as well. This revelation, if widespread enough, could bring a heavenly revolution. Such a precious but simple formula to happiness! This is the high road!

Ask, and it shall be given to you.

MATTHEW 7:7

For everyone who asks receives.

MATTHEW 7:8

Render . . . unto God the things which be God's.

LUKE 20:25 (KJV)

Freely ye have received, freely give.

MATTHEW 10:8 (KJV)

Truly, truly, I say to you, a slave is not greater than his master; neither one who is sent greater than the one who sent him. If you know these things, you are blessed if you do them.

JOHN 13:16-17

However much we shared our spiritual life, however much we served Him together, Nancy found countless other occasions to serve Him, alone and in secret. It would have been unlike

44

her to waste the days and weeks that my career kept us apart. She was not one to wait for my initiative, but especially in spiritual matters she was quick to act. And so she made a multitude of investments, many in secret and known only to the Lord to this day. Nancy knew it didn't take money to serve, just love and those spare moments that are in the days of even His busiest children.

In the days following her death, among the many cards, letters, and calls, I saw more clearly than ever before the influence of one dedicated life. I discovered how often she had written letters of cheer to elderly friends living alone. At each of the three cities in which we lived, she had discovered how much a young heart could do to cheer the lives of the aged and infirm. She frequently visited them and found a myriad of things to do for them, but nothing cheered them more than her radiant countenance and effervescent spirit. And as we moved on, from one city to the next, she didn't forget but simply enlarged her correspondence.

Only God can measure the ultimate value of Nancy's contribution to the life of a young woman who wrote me that she would never have completed college but for the encouraging letters she received from Nancy. And so it was with young people. How she cheered them on! If a young person shared her great musical talent and committed it to our Lord, that young person inevitably became a very special project—the subject of much prayer, frequent words of encouragement, and constant readiness to help. Youth choirs had an instant sponsor in her. It's no coincidence that the music program in every church in which she served prospered.

When anyone did something for Nancy, it never occurred to her that often they were doing what they were paid to do. Every kindness to her formed an affectionate bond. She knew no casual acquaintances. The best example I recall of this facet of her loving nature was an occasion about three weeks after the birth of our third child, when she busied herself in the baking of four pies and then delivering one each to the obstetrician, to his nurse, to his receptionist, and to the pediatrician. This was her way of saying "thank you" and, as unique as it might seem, is exactly what those who knew Nancy best would expect of her.

Nancy especially loved little people. She grieved for those who had no one to care for them, and she tried in every little way to compensate. One of the first questions our children asked after the funeral was, "And who's going to take Mary to school?" "Who's Mary?" I asked, only to learn that none of them knew except that their mother had discovered her walking farther

46

to school than most of today's children walk, and had immediately arranged to transport her along with her own brood. An older woman also stopped by to pay tribute to Nancy, saying that she had first met her when Nancy stopped once to give her a ride.

But I believe the most tearful tribute paid, and the one that touched me most, was that of a little Mexican housemaid who served a family across the street. After the funeral, when the crowds were gone, she appeared at our door with tear-stained cheeks. I took her hand in mine, and we wept together for a precious moment. And she left. This language of grief and love was the only language we shared. For she spoke not a word of English, nor I of Spanish. But I knew that Nancy had often asked her over for a cup of tea and a brief rest from her long day's work. Only our precious Lord knows how they ever managed to communicate, but they were dear, dear friends.

So many were the daily investments of our Nancy that I could scarcely chronicle the ones I'm aware of. Only God knows the ultimate worth of Christian acts of kindness, and it's my deep conviction that the returns from billions of dollars spent by governments in the name of welfare can never match the worth of the invest-ments of love made by God's children after the fashion of this one. And Nancy is but the one known best to me. Service seems to come naturally from the woman who follows Christ—more so, it seems, than from man. In these days when women's lib is a favored topic, I think of Nancy and how free she was. But that freedom meant far more to her than is evident in the chants of today. And what a transformed world this would be if every believer today could find Nancy's passion: freedom really means "the freedom to serve God and man."

And I heard a voice from heaven, saying, "Write, 'Blessed are the dead who die in the Lord from now on!'" "Yes," says the Spirit, "that they may rest from their labors, for their deeds follow with them."

REVELATION 14:13

5

Death

O DEATH, WHERE IS YOUR VICTORY?
O DEATH, WHERE IS YOUR STING?

1 CORINTHIANS 15:55

Death is perhaps the most feared word in the language of man, for it speaks of the unknown. Our modern media, particularly television, has explored many unknowns in our time. Sitting in our own living rooms, we have seen the secrets of space exposed and have set our eyes on the moon. We have had the opportunity to hear and see the firsthand reactions of men experiencing the once unknown sensations of weightlessness and of unbelievable speed. Most of us by now have received firsthand descriptions of experiences only imagined until our time and of events even as they unfolded. We have successfully assaulted the unknown until man, confusing conquest with creation, has begun to think of himself as God.

But there is one vast unknown which continues to haunt man, for no one has appeared on our screens to say, "This is how I found death." No one has suited himself in a million dollars' worth of special gear and stepped across the threshold of death to gather data for a world holding its breath. Although some have made elaborate advance plans and painstaking arrangements, there have been no authenticated messages sent back by those on the other side of death. As one fearful unknown after another falls to man's ingenuity, this remaining unknown grows increasingly ominous. Every man knows that he must experience it for himself; so, in typical ostrich fashion, man lives as though he shall never die. Thus he hides from himself the surest truth he knows.

It's interesting to observe the excitement generated by talk of the population explosion. This is an acceptable subject for two reasons: (1) men believe resolutely that the answer will be found in time to avert catastrophy and (2) if the answer is not found, the individual expects to survive what the masses cannot. The ecological crisis, with all the horrors of worldwide pollution, is an acceptable and popular subject for the same reasons. And likewise war, famine, and natural disasters. None of these has the impact of death itself, as a personal experience.

Who can deny that, in 120 years (if the Lord tarry), all of today's three-billion-plus inhabitants of earth will be dead? Not a third, not one half, not even 90 percent, but all of us are going to succumb to a simple event that cannot be altered: the passage of time. Confronted by this crisis, man no longer feels like God. He knows, instead, that he is utterly and completely helpless.

The admission to oneself of the inevitability of death, one's own physical death, is the entranceway to maturity. A life that fails to take death into account has a shallowness that robs the owner of life's and death's greatest victories. Does one plan a trip without a destination? Can a race be run without a finish line? And how can one hope to lead a mature life without considering inevitable death? Yet, all indications are that most deaths are unplanned, unexpected, and unwanted.

The central figure in a death event has no choice, of course, but to accept it when it comes—if not mentally, certainly physically. The bystander, however near and dear or however distant, might react in any number of ways. The death reactions displayed by those who know and love the deceased speak volumes about the departed and about the survivors. Being so near the center of the death event of Nancy provided me with a personal insight that intensified my view of her life. At the same time it stripped all pretense from the lives of those who loved her; and, as it laid bare their response to death, it demonstrated the needs and the strengths of their own lives.

To note so many deeply spiritual friends as they tempered our fresh sorrow and genuine love with unashamed rejoicing over Nancy's victory, to laugh and cry with them, and to give thanks together was an experience that only God's children can possibly understand. On the contrary, so many on the fringes, even though secure in the faith and themselves heaven-bound, yet lacked the maturity to cushion the truth of her passing with the greater truth of her victory. Her whole life spoke of this ultimate victory, and it was difficult to see how anyone could reject her death, knowing that to do so was to reject her blessed life as well. How could one thrill to her race of life and not rejoice in her victory at the finish line?

I have suffered the loss of all things, and count them but rubbish in order that I may gain Christ, and may be found in Him, not having a righteousness of my own derived from the Law, but that which is through faith in Christ, the righteousness which comes from God on the basis of faith, that I may know Him, and the power of His resurrection and the fellowship of His sufferings, being conformed to His death; in order that I may attain to the resurrection from the dead.

PHILIPPIANS 3:8*b*-11

These are Paul's words, of course, but they are Nancy's words as well to all those who knew her spirit and who know her Lord. They well know that Nancy, as Paul, now has her heart's great desire and glories in the presence of our Lord.

The great numbers of those who understand Nancy, her life and her death, comprise a beautiful testimony to her. As one aged, bedridden woman, so often ministered to by our Nancy, put it, "If not Nancy, then who?" Her life was well planned by her and God, and death was not a whispered fear. Typical of her was her eagerness in life to discuss her own death and her accompanying reluctance to consider the death of those she loved.

It was a beautiful and moving experience to speak and pray with Nancy a few years ago as she left the deathbed of her saintly and beloved grandmother. She spoke eloquently of the angels

53

that filled the room, and she was as aware of them as her grandmother must have been when she whispered to her beloved daughters and to Nancy, "I'm going now." With a smile she departed this world in the company of that band of angels, to be borne to the very presence of our Lord.

True, Nancy's departure was far more violent and sudden; but, when our son spoke to her in the debris of the tragic accident and asked, "Are you all right, Mother?" she nodded, and left. And indeed, she was and is all right.

But what of the others? There are those who rejected her death, who looked for answers that eluded them. Some said it was unfair, even accusing God. Calls came from distant places, carrying a single, bitter question: Why? One letter came from a close friend, saying he was unable to sleep for his inability to answer the question, What if it were my wife? I found my oft-repeated assurance, "She's all right." All right indeed, in a state far exceeding in glory any that we can even imagine.

Or do you not know that all of us who have been baptized into Christ Jesus have been baptized into His death? . . . For if we have become united with Him in the likeness of

54

His death, certainly we shall be also in the
likeness of His resurrection.

ROMANS 6:3, 5

One with Christ! Our Nancy is one with Christ this very day. Can we weep for her? Only with tears of joy. Can we weep for ourselves? Only if we refuse to face death, rejecting it until there remains no choice. How much better it is to face death early in life. Nancy accepted death years ago when she elected to share Christ's death and hence His resurrection. Having made this election, she lived a joyful life of service and was called home to those mansions of glory where even now she goes on living more gloriously than ever before.

This simple truth of heaven is published in every language and described in a multitude of ways. The truth is too often embellished, frequently concealed by forms of religion; yet it is the heart of God's Good News. It says simply that we must be born again or face the second death. It's the law of three: two births and one death, or one birth and two deaths. God authored the law and gives man the choice. Man must think on it; and if he is to choose wisely, he must consider death. Nowhere, even in God's own Word, is the offer more clearly or more eloquently stated than,

For God so loved the world, that He gave His only begotten Son, that whoever believes in Him should not perish, but have eternal life.

JOHN 3:16

That which is born of the flesh is flesh; and that which is born of the Spirit is spirit. Do not marvel that I said to you, "You must be born again." The wind blows where it wishes and you hear the sound of it, but do not know where it comes from and where it is going; so is every one who is born of the Spirit.

JOHN 3:6-8

And so it is that the flesh that was Nancy died. But the spirit that is Nancy lives and will never die. And when we, through the birth of the Spirit, find that same immortality, then it is that we can face with confidence the inevitable death of the physical body and say with Paul:

But when this perishable will have put on the imperishable, and this mortal will have put on immortality, then will come about the saying that is written, "DEATH IS SWALLOWED UP IN VICTORY? O DEATH, WHERE IS YOUR VICTORY? O DEATH, WHERE IS YOUR

STING?" *The sting of death is sin, and the power of sin is the law; but thanks be to God, who gives us the victory through our Lord Jesus Christ.*

1 CORINTHIANS 15:54-57

6

Time

But do not let this one fact escape your notice, beloved, that with the Lord one day is as a thousand years, and a thousand years as one day.

2 PETER 3:8

God is not, indeed cannot be bound by time. If eternity is without end, then how can it possibly be broken into equal parts? Surely in God's heaven, prepared for us, His children, there'll be no need for calendars or clocks, for what would they measure? Time, the chief limitation of this life, is built of measured units that will be swept away forever with the old heavens and the old earth. Time comes upon us sometimes as friend, sometimes as foe. We hear of the tyranny of time, the ravages of time, and time that heals. So time in itself is a curse to some, a blessing to others. Sometimes it is abundant, too often fleeting. It has no distinguishing single quality but simply constitutes the stage on which man lives out his life, seeking or evading God's truths of life and death.

How varied our perspective when we view this thing called time! To the child, a year is surely an eternity; to that same child grown old, a year is swift and relentless.

When we consider the life of Abraham Lincoln, few of us can recall the number of his earthbound years. We know so well, though, the triumphs of his life and the meaning of it.

So it is that the quality of life rapidly diminishes the importance of its length in years, particularly so in retrospect. What a tragic contradiction that, in our "one nation under God," billions of dollars are spent in the hope of extending human life a few years, while God's Word, which points the way to a timeless, unending life, is systematically withdrawn from our country's institutions. We all know that physical life, however long it may be extended, must end. How much more successful a God-serving life of twenty or thirty years than a fruitless self-serving life of a hundred!

*The days of our years are threescore years
and ten; and if by reason of strength they be
fourscore years, yet is their strength labour*

and sorrow; for it is soon cut off, and we fly away.

PSALM 90:10 (KJV)

In this life the measurement of time is indispensable as a device to give order to society. It is the basis of a system without which there would be complete chaos. History, even biblical history, would lose much of its meaning if it did not convey events and lives in sequence and if it failed to record the passage of time. The tyranny of time lies only in man's misplaced values. How much of his effort, individual and corporate, goes into the adding on of days?

History is replete with the folly of men, from Ponce de Leon, who wasted his numbered days searching for more, hoping to discover the mythical fountain of youth, to the medical scientists of this century who freeze dead patients to await new cures. History records but few men for the number of their days; Methusaleh at 969 was the champion. But even his life did end. Much more does history record the events, the deeds that reflect the quality of life and service, rather than the length of days. So very many of history's great figures lived lives that fell short of "threescore and ten." Foremost of these is our Lord Jesus Christ, who at thirty-three years of age submitted to death that all may live who follow

60

Him. Jesus, even as He conquered death in His resurrection, likewise conquered time itself.

I said in mine heart, God shall judge the righteous and the wicked: for there is a time there for every purpose and for every work.

Ecclesiastes 3:17 (KJV)

"There is a time," and the Creator of all things is the Author of time. The timelessness of God, which we will someday share, is beyond the comprehension of mortal mind. He gave us time to live, to work, to seek and find, to serve, to love, and to prepare for the timeless eternity ahead.

When Nancy died, I found it difficult not to wish that I might go with her at once. My unfinished work with the children was the chief interdiction of that wish. I did long to be with her, but quickly I knew that it was only a matter of time. Most important of all, I knew it must be God's time. Then, as days passed and I gained a fuller realization of my escalated responsibilities, I found my field reversed. I wished for length of days, that I might see even little Carolyn, then but nineteen months old, to maturity. And I knew again that I was minding God's business, as it is He who has numbered my days. And I exchanged my wish for a prayer that He would provide for our children, whatever the number of my days; and I knew He would, and will.

As I thought in those days on the length of life, I considered the victory of Nancy's thirty-eight years. They were victorious because it was not her way to wait. She was instant to love our Lord and to serve Him. She was ever mindful of opportunities for service to those about her, and always busy for her Lord.

I often recall how sharply I was once brought up on an occasion of meditation. I had for some time considered the question: What would I do if physicians advised me that I had but six months to live? I answered the question with a fantasy. I saw myself racing against time as I passed from friend to friend, speaking of eternal life through simple faith in our Lord Jesus. I saw myself in pulpits, even before civic groups, testifying to the grace of God through His only Son. I saw myself writing feverishly, recording for friend and stranger alike the prospects of glory soon to be mine. Even in my fantasy I felt the weight of responsibility to use those last six months well. It was then, with a start, that I recalled:

> *And Jesus answered and said to him, "It is said, 'You shall not force a test on the Lord your God.'"*
>
> LUKE 4:12

62

My fantasy had been a challenge to God, saying "God, threaten my life, and I will serve Thee
well. Place me under the sentence of early death,
and I'll be Your minister." What had I done?
I had stumbled upon one of the foibles of man,
one that denies to the Kingdom the energies of
countless millions of His children who unthink-
ingly postpone their service. We are too often
thoughtful of Him only when we anticipate life's
end. Six months indeed! And I knew at once
the shallowness of my service, and I knew why
and by whom I had been brought upon the question.

I've had several years since that encounter,
and I hope I've since done at least six months'
work for our Lord. Each month of Nancy's adult
life was a month for the Lord. A life so spent is a
success, be it for thirty years or a hundred.

The deception of time is nowhere more evident than in our young people as they claim the
presence of a generation gap. I hear my own
children say, "Daddy, it's different now," as
though we didn't live in the same world, serving
the same Lord. There is a gap between my great-
grandfathers and me, as they were deceased before my birth. Far from there being a gap between my children and me, there is a blessed
overlap. Being twenty-seven years older than
Marcia, our oldest, if I attain "threescore and

ten," we will have shared forty-three years of history—most of both of our lives. And where, then, is the gap? Marcia has, in fact, shared over eighteen years with three of her four grandparents. Whither the gap?

There is another gap, of course. Our youth are afflicted by it, and youth have known the affliction through the ages. It is not based on time, however, but rather is a matter of missing influence. Yes, a gap, a chasm, or even a pit confronts parents who fail to demonstrate to their children a victorious life, and it confronts children who refuse to observe and consider the higher paths.

Still, there *is* an influence—a negative, overwhelming influence. Narcotics and alcohol that numb and stupefy young minds spell financial success to adult purveyors. Pornographic books and movies that debase and jeopardize the physical and mental health of the nation's youth swell the bank accounts of adult writers, producers, and businessmen. And drinking parents beget marihuana-smoking, pill-popping sons and daughters. And carousing, partying fathers beget sons proclaiming the virtues of free love. Yes, there is more than enough negative influence.

The gap is really a love gap. Every generation, it seems, is short on the love that reaches out to steady the other generation. But there is a way to bridge this gap. In countless homes today it is bridged by God-fearing families where His Word is still read, His name still honored, and "love one another" is the tie that binds. It is said,

> *Train up a child in the way he should go: and when he is old, he will not depart from it.*
>
> PROVERBS 22:6 (KJV)

This message is for all mankind, not for just one generation. God's timeless teachings are true, even in a world that changes somewhat with time.

> *Jesus Christ is the same yesterday and today, yes and forever.*
>
> HEBREWS 13:8

This same Jesus is the Lord of every generation.

And what is time to those who have gone to be with our Lord? Does our Nancy long for us? For her family? Her friends? I am satisfied that from the other side it shall be as though we step across that great divide immediately after her. For with her, as with God, a thousand years shall be as one day. If we can but imagine ourselves as moving through time, rather than time past us, then it is that we can begin to comprehend:

"I am the Alpha and the Omega," says the
Lord God, *"who is and who was and who is
to come, the Almighty."*

REVELATION 1:8

Our omnipresent God can and does survey the
past, the present, and the future. He moves freely through the fixed medium we call time; while
we move through it, helpless to speed the clock,
to slow it, or to stop it, as it ticks away our mortal
existence. Those who have gone to be with Him
in His heaven must surely have conquered time.

To find the difference between time's effect
on man and God's power over time is to find the
key that opens our spiritual perception. It is the
key to the age-old theological dispute of pre-
destination. It is the key to the mystery of how
Christ could pay my sin debt before I was. It is
the key to the statement in Scripture:

*That which hath been is now; and that
which is to be hath already been; and God
requireth that which is past.*

ECCLESIASTES 3:15 (KJV)

66

7

Resources

Ours is a resource-conscious age of the affluent society. Our ears are massaged with terms such as moral resources, spiritual resources, national resources, financial resources, local resources, etcetera. In each case, the term implies possession of some particular commodity or asset.

The implication is very different, however, when these same adjectives are linked with needs rather than with resources. Man's conditioned reflexes signal the defensive when he hears moral needs, spiritual needs, national needs, financial needs, and local needs. Abundance, such as that in which the people of an affluent society revel, nourishes a self-centered philosophy that accentuates the income and would eliminate the outflow of resources.

The wise man considers the terms together. He considers the need, then the resources, then both. Too often the affluent citizen unfortunately specializes in resources, lacking time or interest in the ample need about him. On the other hand, the less fortunate citizen is often so hypnotized by his need that he fails to consider his resources. Either condition is self-reinforcing, and both are formidable barriers to a normal Christian life. Success, corporate or individual, national or local, hinges on a prudent matching of needs and resources, a balancing of the accounts.

This country's great GNP (Gross National Product) staggers the imagination. No one, it seems, has been able yet to establish or even define its corollary, the GNN (Gross National Need).

There is really no resource without a need, nor is there a need lacking a resource. The real problem is nothing more or less than management.

Even our churches are often inept at matching needs and resources. There is no shortage of churches that accumulate resources that they might pursue greater resources. There are churches so conscious of needs that they fail to lift their eyes to the abundant resources. Happy is the church that sees the needs all about, thanks God the Provider, then enthusiastically goes to work for God's glory. Such a church has found the high road to worthy ministries.

Any person so fortunate as to be counted among the participating membership of a ministering church will almost invariably find the same exciting success formula dominating his own life. His spiritual life will be energized; and he'll discover practical applications for business, professional, and social success.

Nancy and I claimed, among our many resources, successive memberships in two truly great churches: Travis Avenue Baptist Church in Fort Worth and Hyde Park Baptist Church in Austin. The dynamic spirit of service prevailing in these two churches, the unfailing leadership of God's Spirit through their able pastors, the excited, joyous participation of their pastors, and the excited, joyous participation of God-loving members lead them consistently into accomplishments for our Lord that are only dreamed of by most churches. And in both cases, the pattern of this great success has involved the matching of resources and needs. In either church, even a casual observer will note the pastor, his staff, and members busily applying God's cornucopia of resources to plentiful needs, at the same time searching hopefully for more and greater needs, and all the time calling them opportunities.

It's a common weakness of man, in this day as in times past, to magnify his own needs and overlook the needs of others, and at the same time to exaggerate the resources of others and fail to see his own. This is sheer covetousness.

> *The desire of the slothful killeth him; for his hands refuse to labour. He coveteth greedily all the day long: but the righteous giveth and spareth not.*
>
> PROVERBS 21:25-26 (KJV)

It seems at first blush a paradox that the sin of covetousness should affect the rich as well as the poor. A common and well-known peeve of the covetous rich man is that the poor man covets his riches. Covetousness, or greed, is restricted to no single economic environment but thrives in every part of the city. It is a one-way sickness, a focus on the self with little or no real concern for others.

On the other hand, a simple Christian view of needs and resources, unselfishness, an open generosity, a respect for possessions of others, and a concern for their needs are likewise not restricted to a single economic environment. Some of God's most destitute children demonstrate a victorious and touching generosity in sharing their meager possessions, just as some wealthy and notable Christian philanthropists have been generous with their plenty.

"Well done, good and faithful slave; you were faithful with a few things, I will put you in charge of many things; enter into the joy of your master."

MATTHEW 25:23

The world looks greedily on a man's accumulated resources and measures him as small or great. God looks on the use a man makes of his resources, be they few or many, and measures the man as great or small. Thus does God measure our faithfulness.

In the first cold dawn following our great tragedy, after the first morning's rising in the knowledge of Nancy's absence, there was a sudden rush of awareness of needs and resources intermingled. God didn't drop a sinker on me without a stronger float. I had His promise of sufficiency, and He put it in my heart to thank Him for needs as well as resources.

And God is able to make all grace abound to you, that always having all sufficiency in everything, you may have an abundance for every good deed.

2 CORINTHIANS 9:8

In that simple text is the greatest resource of man, the passkey to God's treasure-house. From

71

that infinite wealth spring more resources than we can use or even count.

The needs rushed into sharp focus, grim and all but overwhelming in their enormity yet definable and easily assessed. There was the great compelling need to carry out the dreams Nancy and I had fashioned together. These dreams included the successful rearing of our children, a ministry of lives shared with our friends and loved ones, and service to God and man. Added to these needs was the need to honor Nancy's memory and somehow continue her rich ministry of love and compassion, and the really important needs were accounted for. And I knew that to whatever extent these needs were met they would grow, not vanish, and that I would never be without opportunity or purpose in the new life role that was so abruptly thrust upon me.

Months of crushing loneliness taught me the joy of counting the growing needs so long as I could see them as expanding opportunities. I found the blessed truth that it is in times of greatest need that I am drawn closest to Christ, for that is where He is, at the very heart of my need.

> *Jesus answered and said to them, "It is not those who are well who need a physician, but those who are sick."*
>
> LUKE 5:31

72

So I found an increasing awareness of the presence of God from the first moment of Nancy's death and continuing to this moment. In the realized need and in the sharp awareness, the resources have been abundantly revealed. The prime resource, God's nearness, was followed by the resources of loved ones closer than close, of friends filled with wisdom, love, and understanding, and even of unknown friends who cared because they know God and have grown somewhat like Him. The necessary material resources were no problem as long as my health resource remained. The faith of the children and their understanding ways were and are great resources. I soon began to realize that all that ever came my way came as resources. Every possession, every experience, every accomplishment, every thought is a resource. One of the great questions of life is What shall I do with my resources?

Or do you not know that your body is a temple of the Holy Spirit who is in you, whom you have from God, and that you are not your own? For you have been bought with a price: therefore glorify God in your body.

1 CORINTHIANS 6:19-20

You do not belong to yourselves, but to God:

there lies the answer. I have no resources, only the use of them; for they are His and I am His. How then are the resources to be used, if not for Him? Apply the simple test: Is the need worthy of His resources? If it is worthy, meeting the need will please God and glorify Him.

As the days passed, I found higher meaning in my own life. God made me a soldier that I might bear some influence with that hardy breed of man. He made me an engineer that I might win audience with fellow engineers and with those who dream dreams then build them. And he allowed me to suffer crushing loss that I might have identity with the sorrowful and the lonely, that I might understand.

I think so often of a dear lifelong friend, who as a young man found his way into the unfortunate state of alcoholism. After years of fervent prayer and counsel, Nancy and I saw him restored to respectability and to family. I remarked to him in retrospect that I hoped he would himself have the opportunity to help some other alcoholic on the tedious road back. I'll never forget his reply: "Charlie, if I do, it'll be different. I'll understand that alcoholic as you never really understood me because you have never been one." I pray often that my friend has by now turned his old need into a resource for others and for God.

Considering the events of life and their meaning, I found fresh identity with Paul and understood his writing,

I have become all things to all men, that I may by all means save some.

Whatever the events of my life, they identify me with someone and open the doors of their need to God's resources in my keeping. God means for me to use the joyful and sorrowful events of life to glorify Him. He wants my victories and my defeats. He wants me strong and He wants me weak. In all this rush of discovery, I remembered one of Nancy's favorite prayers: "Lord, make me usable." That is to say, "Lord, take me and my need, and make of me Your resource."

To win this perspective of life is to attain true victory, for in it lies a whole new life claimed exclusively by those who openly accept the lordship of Jesus Christ. It is not a life without sorrow, without pain, or without trial and hardship. Though it greatly increases one's prospects, it does not promise social or business success. It does promise this one thing: a victorious life with resources more than sufficient to meet every need. It promises the matchless satisfaction of serving God and man. It answers the question of the ages: What's life all about?

The greatest resource I can offer my fellow-man I offer here. And that great resource is the simple story of my fulfilled need. I offer my testimony that your need, if not already fulfilled, can likewise be met by the grace of our Lord Jesus Christ.

8

Marriage and Love

FOR THIS CAUSE A MAN SHALL LEAVE HIS
FATHER AND MOTHER, AND SHALL CLEAVE TO
HIS WIFE; AND THE TWO SHALL BECOME ONE
FLESH.

MATTHEW 19:5-6

Marriage is regarded variously as an institution, a custom, a game, a punishment, an arrangement, and sheer foolishness. A repeating fact of history is the parallel movements of society to and from God and social customs to and from a respect for the bonds of marriage.

Civilization could, of course, exist without marriage, just as it could exist without civil government. In either case the result would be anarchistic chaos. God did not ordain either marriage or government as a penalty or as a burden but lovingly bestowed them on mankind as a framework for order and social progress. As

77

marriages and governments become increasingly transient, the world's problems grow more and more complex; and as marriage and government are discarded, so are the hopes for a stable society.

It is so much a part of the normal human experience that our minds reject outright the sterile proposal of hedonists that civilization has outgrown its need for marriage. This would, of course, be regression to illiterate tribes existing at near animal levels.

Marriage is meant to be a high and lofty experience, spanning most of our earthbound years. Unfortunately this is too often not the case, for there is no magic in the ceremonial rites, no mysterious miracle in the speaking of the vows.

The miracle is not in the marriage but in the hearts of one man and one woman who determine, with God's help, to be one. And the miracle radiates outward to friends, to family and later to children of the union. One simple word governs the success or failure of marriage, and that word is *love*. In some cases one partner may possess enough love for both; in some, there is not enough love for either. When husband and wife follow the divine purposes, there is love for both and to spare. Successful marriages are turned outward, so that much of the satisfaction afforded the fortunate couple is in seeing the benefits radiating to others.

Where love reigns, it is unbounded. A man and a woman cannot know God-instilled love for one another and then build a fence around that love. Their mutual love will overflow to motivate their children, their families, and all with whom they associate.

Is marriage forever? Certainly not. To insist that it is appeals only to the romantic or sentimental nature of man and denies the teachings of Christ. The Sadducees, it is recorded, sought to trap Jesus with a hypothetical question concerning a woman who had been married in succession to seven brothers, each of whom, in turn, left her widowed.

In the resurrection therefore whose wife of the seven shall she be? For they all had her.

MATTHEW 22:28

Jesus made it very plain that, though marriage is an institution given of God, it is nevertheless earthbound.

But Jesus answered and said to them, "You are mistaken, not understanding the Scriptures, or the power of God. For in the resurrection they neither marry, nor are given in marriage, but are like angels in heaven."

MATTHEW 22:29-30

Marriage itself is temporal. But the love that comes of God transcends time and the grave. It is this relationship, love, that will dominate all our heavenly reunions. And this love does not wait for that heavenly homecoming, for God gives it now to each of His children, even as we enter His promise of eternal life. This gateway we enter, not at the time of physical death but when we die to death and sin and become His forever.

Can love endure forever? Indeed it can! And, if we follow after Jesus Christ and dwell with Him beyond the grave, it not only can but shall prevail forever. To limit such love to marriage is a narrow view indeed. The true love that unites the lives of a Christian man and woman is not so different from the love that binds all Christiandom together. Married love is, of course, more intense and nurtured in an environment quite apart from any other. It is, nevertheless, that same love that the Master taught us when He said,

> *This is My commandment, that you love one another, just as I have loved you. Greater love has no one than this, that one lay down his life for his friends. You are My friends, if you do what I command you.*
>
> JOHN 15:12-14

I have found no problem with certain questions I understand have haunted many freshly widowed Christians. Will I know her in heaven? Of course! Will I love her? Certainly! Will we live as husband and wife? That is a ridiculous notion firmly put down by Christ Himself!

In view of these things, then, what happened to the miracle of two become as one when Nancy died? I'm sure I immediately loved her more, not less; but she was no longer my wife, having risen infinitely above that. And, as I turned back down memory lane, I realized she had long been more to me than a wife. She had always disliked the term *housewife*, much preferring *homemaker*, which she was, and still more. Yes, I lost my wife forever, but I did not lose the person of Nancy. It was and is the person, the individual unique in all the universe, that mattered then and matters yet. I am deprived of contact with Nancy for a time, but we'll be back in touch. And thus it is with all our loved ones who rest in the Lord. The marriage is over; the love goes on forever.

As the lonely days marched by, I was increasingly impressed with the uniqueness of each human being, the individuality, the kindness; and I marveled at so vast a creation, with billions of souls, all different. What a mighty Creator! What love to give individual attention to every one of us! There is no stereotype, no carbon copy production line of like creatures that one might be led to expect as the product of systematic evolution. As I thought of the individuality of Nancy, as even she is known to me with my limitations, I knew how much more an individual she is to our unlimited and loving God, and how He knows and watches over me. And I knew more deeply than ever before the great unmerited love of God for each individual. This same God gave His only Son to die for me, as for you.

It was said by one who meant well that it was so unfair that our particular marriage should be shattered so early and so abruptly by death. When I asked why this one thought the tragedy unfair, the response was, "Because it was such a good marriage." So I meditated on this thought. Yes, it was a good marriage, approaching perfection because God, being love, was in it.

It was unfair, in a sense, for the other driver to fail to see Nancy's car in time. In no other context can I accept the term *unfair*. Tragic, yes; but, in God's permissive will, not unfair.

And I thought to compare a tragically concluded good marriage with the conclusion of a failed marriage. Our children answered this question after a few months as they commented on a wrecked marriage nearby. They were very touched by the sorrow and confusion of a young friend whose parents parted in bitterness and anger. I'll always remember one of our daughters saying, "Isn't that sad, Daddy? It was so much better the way our family was broken."

What faith, and what wisdom! This little one had discovered the power of love, the security of the believer, and the emptiness of hate. As I looked on our children, I knew that Nancy and I had received mighty blessings worthy of a lifetime in just fifteen years.

I believe that many marriages fail because of the romantic fairy tales surrounding love, courtship, and marriage. The concept that for every boy there's a girl and the young girl's dream that somewhere there is the handsome young lover destined to charge into her life make nice fairy tales. But these also lead the young and even not-so-young to count on a magic spell to make marriage succeed.

The successful marriage is fueled by work, by mutual understanding, by unselfish commitment, and—most of all—by a genuine love that, though it may begin as a tiny spark, grows slowly and surely to a respectable and dependable fire that warms the marriage. Sometimes the flame burns more brightly, and occasionally it may flicker briefly. But it burns always because two who care will tend it constantly; and, if one partner falters, the other will work the harder to make love burn all the brighter.

I am a born romantic, yet I cannot reject reality. However much I love Nancy, I know that she was not my one hope for a happy marriage. And I was not her one hope. Both of us would have found happiness separately had we never become aware of one another's existence. However, even if it were possible, I'd never trade those fifteen happy years. But one reason they were so happy was our mutual grasp of reality. I always knew that I was not indispensable to her, that she could live without me, in happiness and with success. She knew the same of me. God had certainly given us that resilience. So only death ended the courtship, as I still struggled to persuade her that no one in the world could love her more or make her happier than I. And she did the same for me. And that was the secret of our almost perfect marriage.

9

Judgment

We could scarcely consider the death of a loved one without considering that one's fate. Nancy and I had long known the comforting promise of the Scriptures with regard to our sin debts, and I never felt concern for her as I reviewed the promise,

> *God was in Christ reconciling the world to Himself, not counting their trespasses against them, and He has committed to us the word of reconciliation.*
>
> 2 CORINTHIANS 5:19

Thanks to the sacrificial love of God's only Son, Nancy's record is clear, and she is safe from this judgment. I know too that there is to be a judgment of our works and that this judgment is to be a joyous occasion, not a fearful one. And I know that all who love the Lord will be gathered for this occasion at the end of the age. This judgment is not going to be in a somber courtroom setting but will be more like the festive celebration of the victors in a sporting event as they approach the judge's stand. There'll be no losers there. Certainly the rewards will vary from saint to saint—some being very great and some very small. How else should I hope to compare my heavenly rewards to those due the early Christian martyrs?

The most compelling thought I have entertained in behalf of Nancy's reward is the knowledge that the judgment of our works is postponed until the end of time. The logic of this postponement is that Nancy's works go on and will continue down through the years. Her works continue in me, in the children, and in her countless friends as we all are influenced by our walk with her. Our works now are enhanced by her earlier works in ministering to us.

Such a ministry typifies the chain of faith by which the Church is propagated through the ages. Only God knows how many saints served as links in the faith chain that brought me to a knowledge of His way. Our debt is so great to so many, and our only hope of repayment is to continue this chain of faith as we share the Good News. Nancy shared, the faith was propagated through her, and her works go on. A crown of glory awaits her on that great day.

As I have reviewed the question of judgment since our tragedy, I have been impressed that, while God has comforted us with regard to our own judgment and has made ample provision for us, He has spoken to us in another sense about judgment. We concern ourselves so often with our position as the accused, as the subject of judgment, as the defendant, that we seldom realize how frequently in this life we place ourselves behind the bench as judge, or in the position of prosecutor. In this regard God has now given me a greater insight; He has helped me to examine my own life and has revealed fresh truths through these days.

Do not judge lest you be judged yourselves. For in the way you judge, you will be judged; and by your standard of measure, it shall be measured to you.

MATTHEW 7:1-2

The admonishment to refrain from judging is perhaps the most misunderstood and confusing admonishment faced by modern Christianity.

The confusion has led to a weakening of the moral force of the Christian community, as many have confused judgment with discernment. Modern churches display an air of permissiveness because they fear to say "That is wrong!" We're breeding a whole generation of Christian Milquetoasts, too timid to raise their voices for fear of offending the Antichrist. We're so careful not to impose our beliefs on others that we scarcely even reveal them.

The Lord did not say that we should not judge, but that we should not judge others. In fact, we are repeatedly urged by the Scriptures to exercise judgment. I must not judge others; Christ made this crystal clear. If we are to separate right judgment from wrong judgment, our examination should be focused on the I and the others. I must assuredly begin by judging myself.

Test yourselves to see if you are in the faith; examine yourselves! Or do you not recognize this about yourselves, that Jesus Christ is in you—unless indeed you fail the test?

2 Corinthians 13:5

This instruction is, of course, directed to Christians, and the key is that Christ Jesus is in me. The fact is, it is not really for me to judge, but for Christ in me. And what a sad neglect if we fail to exercise this particular judgment, for the Spirit most certainly is able to advise each of us whether we are living in faith. This should be a constantly repeated test if we are to grow in faith. We must never avoid such a test for fear of the results, lest we condemn ourselves to spiritual stagnation.

This self-judgment is a closed circuit, for, in fact, the question of my salvation can be known of a certainty only to me and to God. I must accept my fellow Christian on faith, for I cannot intrude into his communication with God. This is why I cannot judge him. For me to judge another, for good or evil, would be to usurp that which belongs to God and to vastly exceed the limits of knowledge and wisdom intrusted to me. As surely as I must avoid judging others, I must not fail in self-judgment, through the power of our Lord.

But judgment most assuredly does not end with ourselves. Indeed, this is but the beginning. Unless we judge needs, we can hardly walk as God wills us to walk.

But examine everything carefully; hold fast to that which is good; abstain from every form of evil.
1 THESSALONIANS 5:21-22

We hear every excuse for tolerating evil, but none of them can circumvent this instruction.

Do you not know that we shall judge angels?
How much more, matters of this life?

1 CORINTHIANS 6:3

The implications of our future roles as judges
of angels is staggering, but how different we shall
be when we assume that responsibility. The
things of this life we are to judge in this life. We
are to be discriminating, practicing the faith we
profess. And nowhere are we told to keep this
judgment secret. Certainly these judgments are
a vital part of our witness to the world.

But now you also, put them all aside: anger,
wrath, malice, slander, and abusive speech
from your mouth. Do not lie to one an-
other, since you laid aside the old self with
its evil practices, and have put on the new
self.

COLOSSIANS 3:8-10*a*

Again, the inference is that the judgment we
are to exercise is turned inward. We are to judge
wrongdoing, wrong attitudes, wrong thinking in
our own lives, both individually and collectively.
As we judge together, as Christians, we can only
grow stronger.

Do you not judge those who are within the
church? But those who are outside, God

judges. Remove the wicked man from among yourselves.

1 CORINTHIANS 5:12b-13

The admonishment is not to take the sinner out of your group, or there would soon be no group. The evil man, though, can only disrupt the Lord's work. To break fellowship with such a one is not to judge him but to judge his deeds as harmful to the Lord's work. No church sensitive to God's Word would allow a known degenerate to teach a Bible class in that church. Could such discernment be thought of as forbidden judgment? It is a judgment of his deeds, not his soul, and of the unpleasant results. In fact, an effective church Bible-teaching program must be staffed by teachers whose talents, desire to serve, and example have come under the judgment of the fellowship, probably through a committee procedure. If one is rejected as a teacher because of harmful practices in his personal life, has the church gone beyond its authority? Have the members involved in such a rejection been guilty of forbidden judging? Not if the decision is in good faith and rendered by spiritual persons acting out of concern for the things of God.

Do not judge according to appearance, but judge with righteous judgment.

JOHN 7:24

But the natural man receiveth not the things of the Spirit of God: for they are foolishness unto him: neither can he know them, because they are Spiritually discerned. But he that is spiritual judgeth all things, yet he himself is judged of no man.

1 CORINTHIANS 2:14-15 (KJV)

So the place of judgment becomes increasingly clear. With God's help, I judge myself that I might make corrections and become a better, more effective disciple. We, as God's people, must judge ourselves as His servants, seeking from a more perfect fellowship a more effective ministry. Our judgments beyond that must be impersonal. If a brother is caught stealing, we must judge the act, reciting God's commandment: "Thou shalt not steal!" But it is God who must judge the brother. If he has come to God through Jesus Christ and confesses his sin, then the judgment is already clear.

Who will bring a charge against God's elect? God is the one who justifies; who is the one who condemns? Christ Jesus is He who died, yes, rather who was raised, who is at the right hand of God, who also intercedes for us.

ROMANS 8:33-34

How, then, could I *dare* to judge a brother, even as Christ is his Advocate with the Father?

It is up to us, then, to be discerning, to be instructed in the ways of righteousness, and to share knowledge and wisdom. We are to admonish one another in brotherly love. How appropriate it is for us to study together the proper stance of a Christian in today's world. We must strengthen one another, not weaken.

> *Be on your guard! If your brother sins, rebuke him; and if he repents, forgive him.*
>
> LUKE 17:3

> *We are to grow up in all aspects into Him, who is the head, even Christ, from whom the whole body, being fitted and held together by that which every joint supplies, according to the proper working of each individual part, causes the growth of the body for the building up of itself in love.*
>
> EPHESIANS 4:15-16

And therein is the key phrase "through love." If we examine our critical feelings toward a brother, we will likely find love failing; and, if love fails, we convict ourselves of wrongly judging, because judgment is oriented on the person rather than on the deed. If, on the other hand, we find a fault in our brother, and feel sorrow and a deeper love for him because of his demonstrated need, we will then admonish him, help him, and know that we have both become a little more like Jesus.

And so the rightful place of judgment is within the brotherhood, strictly an internal matter. What of the lost man, the outsider? Paul made that very plain:

> *For what have I to do with judging outsiders? Do you not judge those who are within the church?*
>
> 1 CORINTHIANS 5:12

That leaves no room for the self-righteousness we Christians too often feel in the presence of the non-Christian, for that very feeling is itself a judgment. I'm sure that my greatest temptation to judge others is directed toward the world. It is too easy to feel a righteous indignation toward such persons as pornographic dealers, toward those who sell narcotics to young children, toward those who teach revolution and anarchy, toward those who openly defy Christ and His Church. To resist the temptation to judge such persons requires a stern reminder from my innermost self and the constant help of the Holy Spirit.

To be so presumptuous as to offer judgment on the world, a Christian overlooks several key facts. The most important fact he overlooks is that the great sin, the fatal sin, is the rejection of Jesus Christ as Saviour. All other sins, including those that tend to elevate our blood pressure, pale into insignificance.

> *And the witness is this, that God has given us eternal life, and this life is in His Son. He who has the Son has the life; he who does not have the Son of God does not have the life.*
>
> 1 JOHN 5:11-12

If God has judged the lost man and condemned him to eternal damnation, then what contribution would I presume to make? Certainly no greater judgment is to be rendered than that which God has already pronounced. Besides, the fact is that God's Word makes it perfectly clear that such judgment is not ours to offer. A comparison of God's judgment and our own reveals how ridiculous we can be when we blunder into the Judge's seat. How excited should I get over a parking ticket naming a public criminal already on trial for his life for senseless mass murder?

The full realization of the judgment lost men

are under should give us no pleasure. It certainly does not please the Father. This is the very fact that should motivate us, in a spirit of love, to offer the Good News: there is a way out of condemnation.

> "WHOEVER WILL CALL UPON THE NAME OF THE LORD WILL BE SAVED." *How then shall they call upon Him in whom they have not believed? And how shall they believe in Him whom they have not heard? And how shall they hear without a preacher? And how shall they preach unless they are sent?*
>
> ROMANS 10:13-15a

Therein lies the whole answer. God renders the judgment, and He sends His own people to preach the means of escape, of forgiveness. Ours is a ministry of love, to tell of Christ and of the open door to God's forgiveness. Those of us who have come through that door are the very ones on whom God depends to mark that door, to point it out to all who are willing to receive our witness.

I have left unanswered many important questions about secular judgment, criminal and civil courts, war, and man-made laws. A right attitude toward God's will for our lives, while it sets us apart, does not deny us an earthly citizenship. It is not wrong for us to support both the passage and the enforcement of laws to make a better nation, state, and city. I have spoken here of individual judgment, not of the right of man to govern himself. Anyone seeking the right stance in these things would do well to begin with this Scripture:

> *Let every person be in subjection to the governing authorities. For there is no authority except from God, and those which exist are established by God. Therefore he who resists authority has opposed the ordinance of God; and they who have opposed will receive condemnation upon themselves.*
>
> ROMANS 13:1-2

These words would seem sufficient to give pause to any professed Christian bent on revolution by violent or by nonviolent, illegal means.

History has given us an excellent example of how we are to regard evil, even while resisting the temptation to judge its practitioners.

> *He rescued righteous Lot, oppressed by the sensual conduct of unprincipled men (for by what he saw and heard that righteous man, while living among them, felt his righteous*

soul tormented day after day with their lawless deeds).

2 PETER 2:7-8

It is not unusual in our day to see the focus of our misplaced wrath on persons, even as we neglect to condemn the evil.

Judgment takes many forms, some of them being the right, even the duty, of the children of God. I must begin by judging myself. I must share in the corporate judgment exercised by my church. Finally I must judge the things of this life, that I might walk circumspectly. All these judgments must be spiritual in order that they will have their origin from Christ in us.

We must not judge persons, more particularly the outsiders, the lost. And we must not judge in any case from our own wisdom, as though it were sufficient.

To approach the whole question of judgment, I am convinced that we must do so with a full measure of love that passes all understanding. As long as we consciously and conscientiously practice this great love that comes from the Father Himself, we have no need of fear that we might fall prey to the sin of judging others.

10

New Directions

*Be anxious for nothing, but in everything
by prayer and supplication with thanksgiv-
ing let your requests be made known to
God.*

PHILIPPIANS 4:6

The fruitful years that have passed since the
death of our Nancy have been witness to an
aggregation of all of life's superlatives. The
thoughts I have recounted in these pages are by
no means casually recalled, they are not passing
in the sense that they are temporary, nor are
they new truths.

The spiritual discoveries and rediscoveries of
these years have changed my life beyond any previous experience, except for the experience of
salvation by God's own grace. But God has un-
doubtedly planted anew within me truths that
have stood the test of the ages. It is my fervent

prayer that I shall be ever alert to these precious truths and to the needs of those whose paths I may cross through the years. Such living truths need frequent rediscovery; they are heightened by application, they cry out for sharing with the horde of humanity never having known our Lord, and they are the missing dimension of the lives of those on the fringe, those who know Him but don't really seem to care.

I have recounted here some of my innermost thoughts and spiritual discoveries; they have sprung from an experience of tragic proportions that at the same time sensitized my mind and soul to receive the blessings of God. These truths would be blessing enough, but God has seen fit to go beyond, and I cannot end this account without a grateful acknowledgment to Him of some of the great moments in my life since our day of tragedy. Many of these events I count as miracles. Some of them have a great part in my spiritual discoveries, even as I have proved them in practice.

How could I possibly be father and mother to our five children while maintaining the heavy travel schedule my employment required? Nancy and I had prayed for at least three years that God would release me from the particular organization that I had served for all but the first two years of our marriage. In spite of an adequate education, an acceptable professional standing, a willingness to retrench if need be, and a general shortage of qualified professional engineers, it seems there was always something to prevent a change, our many efforts and fervent prayers notwithstanding.

God clearly wanted me where I was, and we both knew it. We knew even as we were required to move from our beloved Fort Worth, where we had spent seven golden years fashioning eternal friendships. We were satisfied that we were in His will. Even had she known the tragedy to befall in Austin, Nancy would never have wanted to challenge God's will. So we had continued in that same employment, knowing that God would make it clear and would open new doors in His own time.

And so it was at her death. I still served as an engineer in a work that had once meant much to me but had long since lost its attraction, except for long cherished associations with men I was proud to look up to. For some, my respect was professional; for others, admiration of one talent or other; and for a few, recognition of spiritual maturity. I had long since tired of weekly travels; for though they took me to good friends, they took me from home and family.

My most immediate need, if I hoped to tend our wounded children, was to put an end to my travel. Such was not possible if I was to remain in the position I held. So I prayed, asking God that He would give me quick relief in the matter. This was little different than the prayer Nancy and I had long prayed; except for the new and greater urgency.

I felt a very sharp sense of need to serve people in some special way. I was so sure that God could use me somehow in housing the poor. Nancy and I had long felt and prayed that my professional career could someday be dedicated to such a ministry, one that would deal with a growing and perplexing problem of our time. And I was sure that He had prepared me with some of the long-sought technical answers with which to meet the need.

But I nevertheless prayed, "Thy will be done." In a very few weeks, God sent the answer. And He directed me, not as I expected but back into public service, this time with the city of Austin. I was so convinced of His direction in the matter that I was not even able to feel disappointment in the surprise answer. He had provided for me and for the children in His own way. I was still given the privilege of serving people, and I continue in my efforts to do so even now in the same position. And yet the call to a greater service haunts me, and I am no less convinced that God has a work for me to do that concerns the many children and adults who have both material and spiritual needs. I yearn to have a part in helping them into adequate family housing and at the same time to an expanded spiritual awareness. It is so crucial that we minister to the whole man.

But this may never be, for it may be the imaginations of my own heart; but, if the desire is of God, He will open the way, and His present provision will have been another step in His preparing me. God so often answers my prayers with "not yet," for He knows whether I am ready.

God has given me honest and rewarding work to do, a place of service, and new and pleasant associations. Some might fail to see God's hand in my career and in my life, but for me the timing is such perfection that I can only credit Him as the pieces fall into place. And I know, too, that God might put me in an office for the purpose of influencing just one person, lost or floundering on the fringes of His Kingdom. It is this happy prospect that makes it so easy to go wherever and to do whatever He directs.

Beyond God's ample and ready provision of material things, of a means for a daily presence with our children, and an opportunity to contribute to society's needs through my work, the long-range implications of a one-parent family began to press upon me early in my aloneness.

There were many relatives as well as friends

who knew no bounds in their willingness to help with the children. The children's acceptance of our new circumstances was a beautiful sermon to the world about them. It told of great faith, courage, and the love of a mother strong enough to span the unknown to comfort and to encourage. It told of a mother who had found the time to teach the important things and to prepare her children for life as it really is.

Still, there is an artificial sense to a home with one parent. God provided us quickly with a live-in housekeeper. Hazel loved the children as her own and served the household well and faithfully, and the children loved her and accepted her quickly. Even locating a housekeeper was counted by some as a minor miracle. Who knows how many little children have suffered as their families have given up after desperate searches for this vanishing specialist? The demand for substitute mothers in our broken society far outstrips the supply. What a magnificent ministry awaits the woman with sufficient time and love to enter the lives of children deprived of the vital mother love.

But God did supply our immediate need, and our fractured family began to mend. Even the younger children, though, began to sense that they had a commercial mother. The distressing feature of this development was the abandonment of hard-won habits, as little ones began to leave their duties to Hazel.

They showed some distress because their substitute mother was an unaccustomed part-time arrangement (5½ days a week). She judiciously preferred to retire early, leaving the family to itself for the evening. Family activities had a missing dimension as we traveled, attended church, and faced so many other routines that had always included Mother.

I became painfully aware that we six plus Hazel, however dedicated she was, would never provide the setting Nancy and I had planned for the rearing of the children. And this awareness marked the beginning of perhaps the most profound miracle of my life.

Confident of God's compassionate understanding, and knowing at the same time that there would be those who would regard it as sacrilege, I began to pray for guidance in the matter of rebuilding a whole family, after only a few months without Nancy. Some would say I dishonored her memory with such a prayer. I was painfully aware of a "customary waiting period," but much more aware of the real need. The most heartening reaction came later from a dear friend of mine, and perhaps Nancy's closest friend, as this understanding woman suggested to me that to even accept the possibility of a second marriage was complimentary to the life that I had shared with Nancy and evidenced her success in building a marriage.

Yes, I consciously and earnestly prayed that, if God could see fit to give me a renewed life with another woman, that He would do so quickly and that she could be a mother to our children as well as a companion to me. I felt keenly that all the children, and especially the girls, must not have time to grow accustomed to being motherless. Every clumsy, mother effort I made convinced me more certainly of the need. In those days I became an ardent supporter of the women who rear our children and still keep judicious silence as we proud fathers receive the compliments for well-bred, intelligent, beautiful children.

Nancy often said she could never remarry if I should leave her, and I think she probably was correct, though I had no objection even then to the idea of remarriage. For that reason I insured myself as heavily as I could, that she could be free to choose a single life in the event of my death and be able to provide for herself and the children without being compelled to seek employment during their early years.

That self-same, selfless Nancy on the same occasions noted that, if she were to leave me, she felt I would surely remarry. The thought made

her sad, but her love shone through. I believe
she considered that likelihood yet another form
of insurance for the children. She most surely
knew that I could never be an adequate mother
to our children.

I prayed, and as I prayed I recalled how all
things are possible with God. And I remembered the admonishment to pray specifically.
For an engineer, the setting out of specifications
comes naturally; and I carefully laid my request
before God.

"God, if You wish me ever to remarry, show me
who she must be. But, Lord, let her be a devout
and faithful Christian, one who believes much as
I do. And please, God, let her be a widow who
had a great love for a good man, that we might
share the knowledge of an earlier love, and that
she might understand the pain of my recent loss.
And let her be the mother of at least one child,
that I may love her child and that she may love
mine until we can see them as ours. Let her be
filled with patience, Lord, and wisdom, and great
energies, for to adopt five children is so much to
ask." I felt almost foolish as I crowned all this
with, "Lord, let her be one who knows and loves
our Nancy." Such a prayer could only have been
prayed by a fool or by a man with faith com-
pounded with realized need.

And miracle of miracles, it happened. He

called my attention to a radiant young woman who had sung beside Nancy in the church choir. As the light of understanding dawned, I remembered Nancy telling me of her exceptional new friend. "A young widow," she had said, "studying at the university for her doctorate in physics." She had been greatly impressed with Page and her unconquerable spirit. They had lunched together two days before Nancy's death, and Nancy had glowed all that evening with the inspiration from her visit with Page.

Widowed for some years, and with little or no intentions of ever remarrying, this indomitable Page was rearing her one son, John, and preparing herself for a meaningful career in physics and in teaching.

She later admitted to simultaneous promptings of God's Spirit. Our romance was a whirlwind, because there was never a doubt where it was headed. Only a year after the tragedy, we stood before our pastor, our six children our only attendants. Our two families were merged into one. The years following have been exciting ones, and the miracle of God's care grows ever greater.

The children have a whole life; and the benefits include the love and wisdom of two exceptional mothers, both of whom have now registered strong and meaningful influences in their lives. Life goes on for us all with zest, with promise, and with love.

We have not entered a new life but into a new chapter. It might be said that we have started all over, but that would be an untruth. For we still hold the past in our hearts, as we live in the present and hope for the future. Christ continues to reign as Head of this house. Our family has remained stable in the face of change because no force can destroy the foundation that is Jesus Christ.

We have received much, and continue to receive. Which leads me daily to say, "And what shall this man do?" Then I know, as life with Christ has already taught, I need make no decision, except that one great decision to follow Him. I must keep the lines open; I must strive to live as much like Him as I can; and I must prepare my mind, body, and soul for whatever He has for me.

I know what I would like to do. This, though, cannot be my motivation, however noble my ambitions may seem to me. Only the doors He opens can lead me to His purposes. He asks from me diligence, awareness, and a constant readiness to perform whatever service He has for me to do. His admonition to me, as to all who would follow Him, is well expressed by Paul:

Therefore be careful how you walk, not as unwise men, but as wise, making the most of your time, because the days are evil. So then do not be foolish, but understand what the will of the Lord is.

EPHESIANS 5:15-17

May God give me sufficient grace to so live.

Epilogue

Why did Nancy have to die?

Perhaps this book, inspired by the beauty of her life and the victory of her death, has served to sharpen your spiritual vision.

Her life's passion was to follow after her Lord Jesus Christ. She would consider it her highest achievement to have died for you, even as He did.